JACK JOHNSON
TO THE SEA

CONTENTS

This book was approved by Jack Johnson

This book was printed on recycled paper, using soy based ink.
To learn more about Jack Johnson's green efforts, please visit JackJohnsonMusic.com/greening, and AllAtOnce.org.

Transcribed by Jeff Jacobson

Cherry Lane Music Company
Director of Publications/Project Editor: Mark Phillips
Project Coordinator: Rebecca Skidmore

ISBN 978-1-60378-276-0

YOU AND YOUR HEART

Words and Music by
Jack Johnson

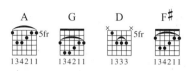

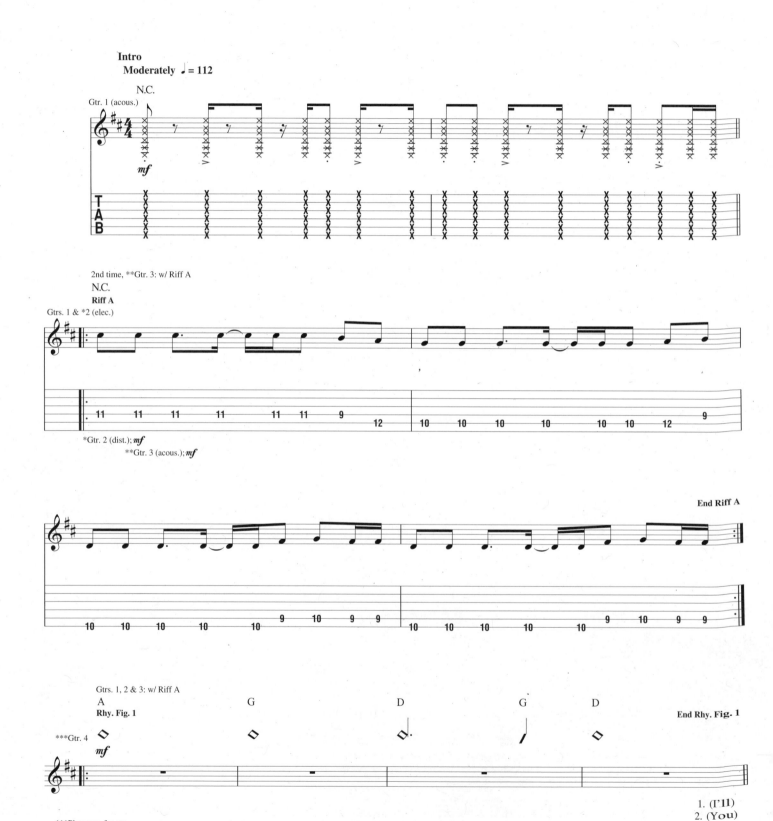

***Piano arr. for gtr.

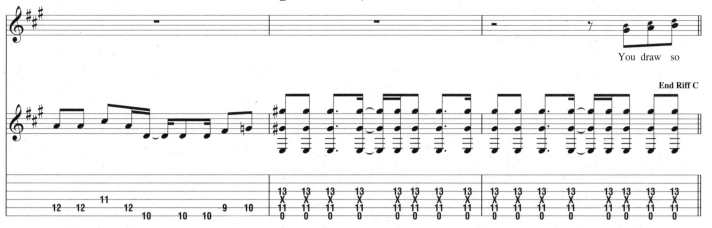

You draw so

Outro
Gtrs. 1, 2 & 3: w/ Riff C (1 2/3 times)

man - y lines in the sand, lost the fin - ger - nails on your hands. How you

gon - na scratch an - y backs? Bet - ter hope the tide will take our lines a -

way. Take all _____ our lines _____ and... _____ Hope the tide will

take our lines a-... Hope the tide will take our lines a -

way. Take all _____ our lines _____ a - way. _____

TO THE SEA

Words and Music by
Jack Johnson

6

8

Guitar Solo

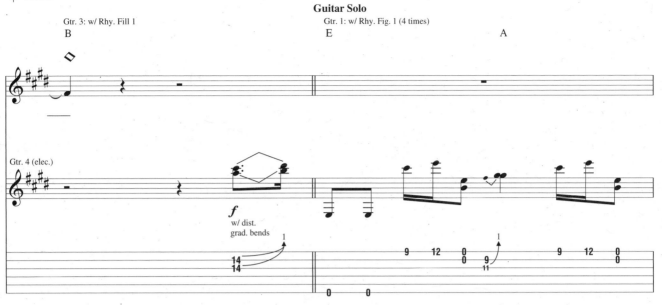

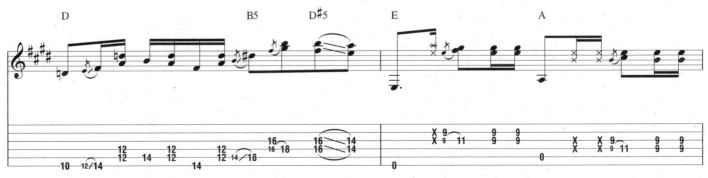

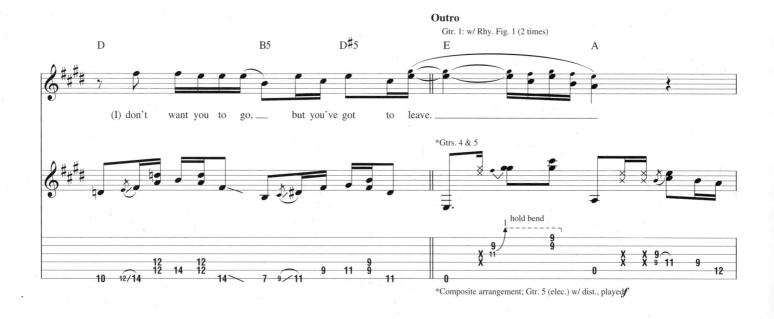

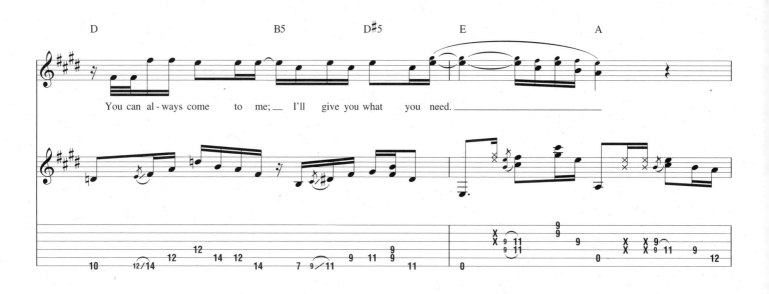

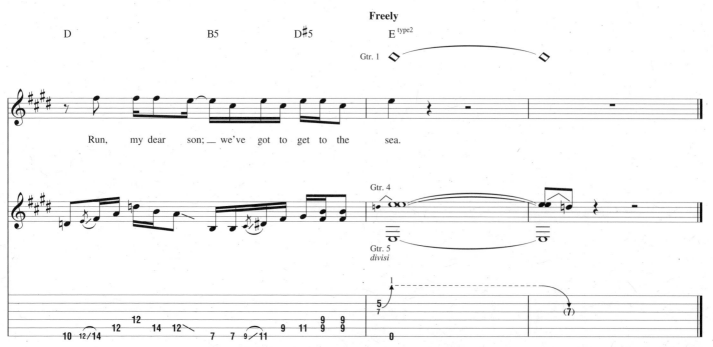

NO GOOD WITH FACES

Words and Music by
Jack Johnson

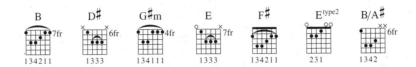

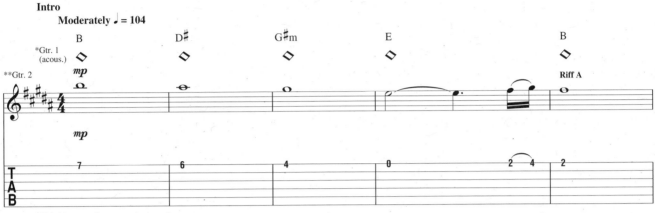

*First 14 meas. of song are piano arr. for gtr.

**Melodica arr. for gtr.

1., 4. No good with fac - es and I'm bad with ___ names. ___

(cont. in notation)

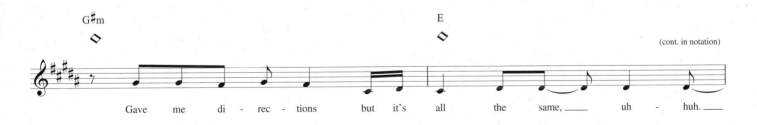

Gave me di - rec - tions but it's all the same, ___ uh - huh. ___

1st time, Gtr. 2: w/ Riff A
2nd time, Gtr. 2: w/ Riff B

I'm lost. I'm too

ti - red to try.

Fine

Verse

Gtr. 2 tacet

2. Street lamps are bro - ken; black the way I came.
3. Road signs were stol - en, left here hold - ing this flame.

Who broke the moon - light? Watch it wax and wane, uh - huh.
Who stole my pa - tience? Who stole my way? Uh - huh.

12

I'm lost. _____ I'm ____ too

ti - red ____ to try. _____

Let's not get a - head _____ of our - selves ____ now.

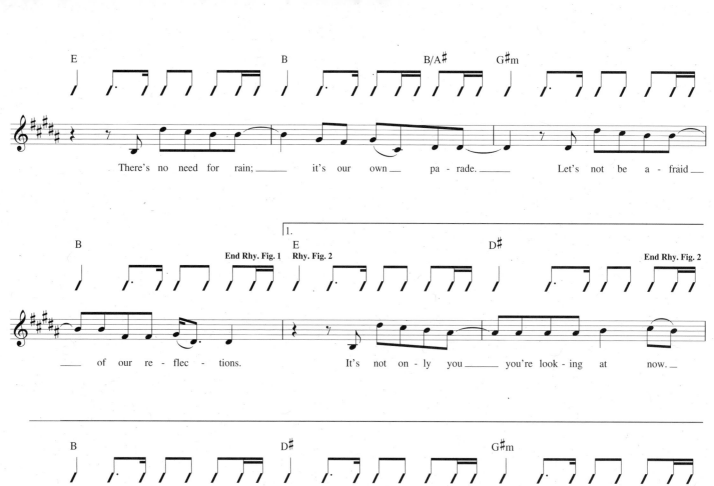

There's no need for rain;_____ it's our own ___ pa - rade._____ Let's not be a - fraid___

___ of our re - flec - tions. It's not on - ly you_____ you're look - ing at now.___

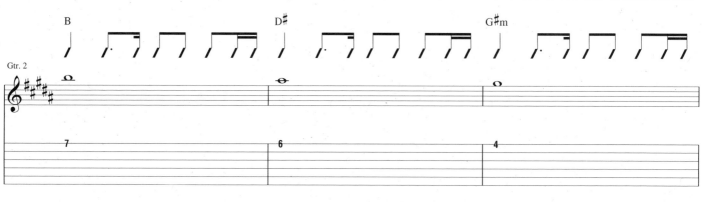

Gtr. 2

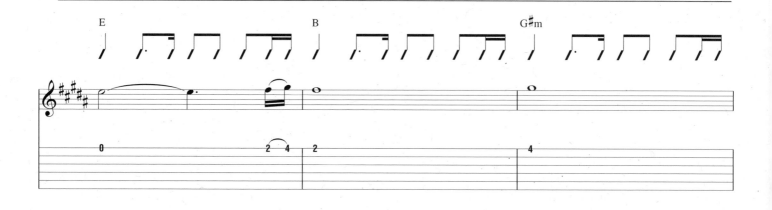

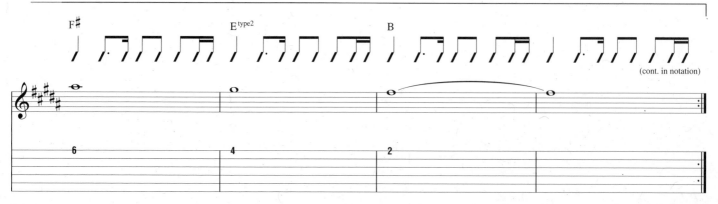

(cont. in notation)

AT OR WITH ME

Words and Music by
Jack Johnson

Guitar Solo

*w/ octaver

*Set for an octave lower   **Chord symbols reflect overall harmony.

D.S. al Coda 2

Oh, oh, oh, oh, oh, oh, oh,

octaver off

Coda 2

Interlude

21

WHEN I LOOK UP

Words and Music by
Jack Johnson

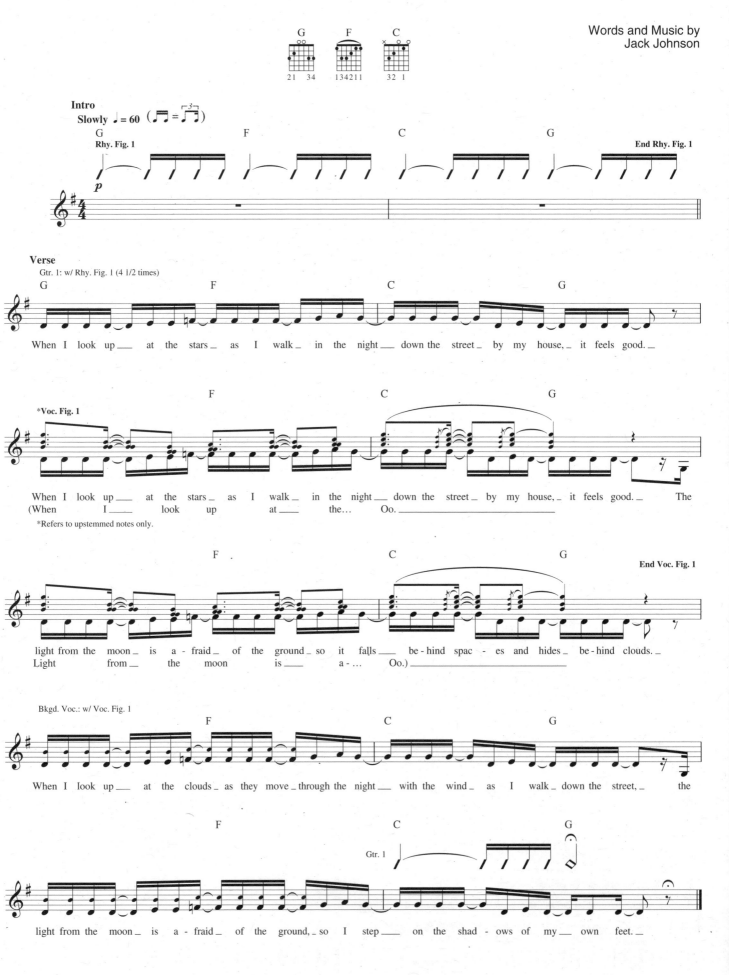

FROM THE CLOUDS

Words and Music by
Jack Johnson

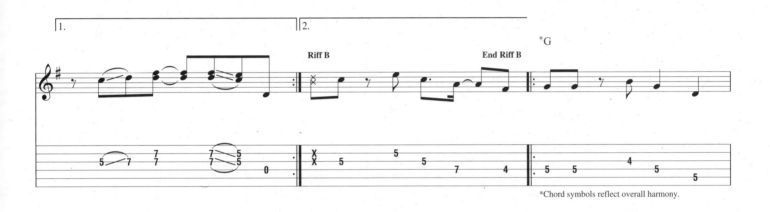

*Chord symbols reflect overall harmony.

when you beat me in dou - ble sol - i - taire.   You're so___ sweet___ to me

D.S. al Coda

in a world that's not al - ways fair.   We could

⊕ Coda

Bridge

The more love___ that___ you feel, _____   the

let ring - - - ⊣

more your lit - tle heart will___ ache. _____   Love's the on - ly thing that car - ries___ on. ___

let ring - - - ⊣   *let ring - -*

It's the on - ly thing this world can't___ take. ___ This love___ is ours. ___

let ring - - - - - - ⊣   *let ring - - - ⊣*   *let ring - - - ⊣*

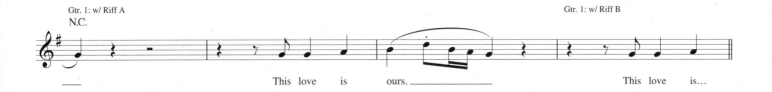

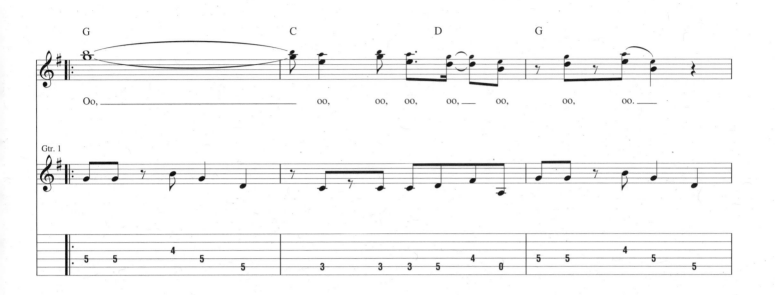

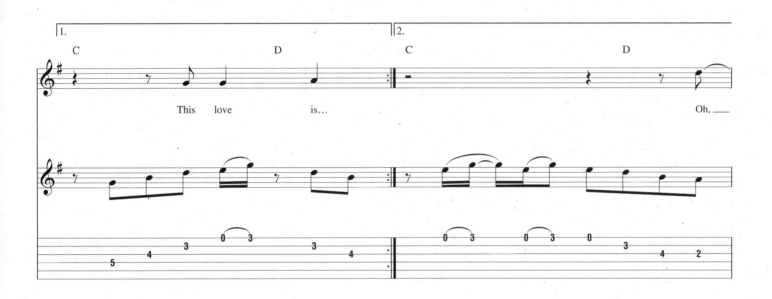

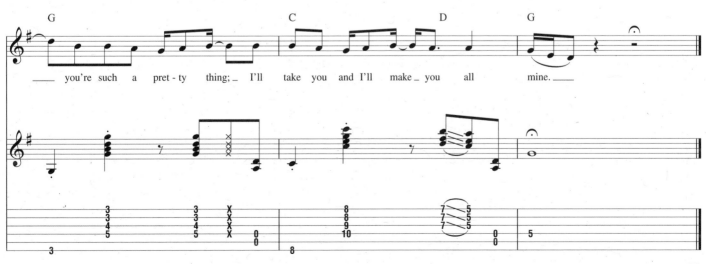

MY LITTLE GIRL

Words and Music by
Jack Johnson

32

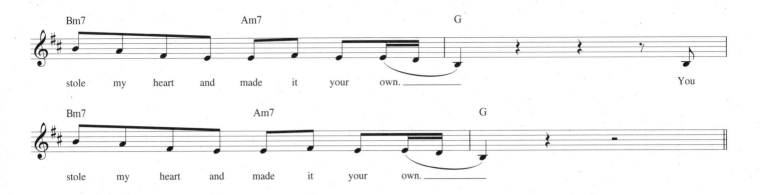

stole my heart and made it your own. _____ You

stole my heart and made it your own. _____

Outro

*Lightly hit strings w/ fingers.

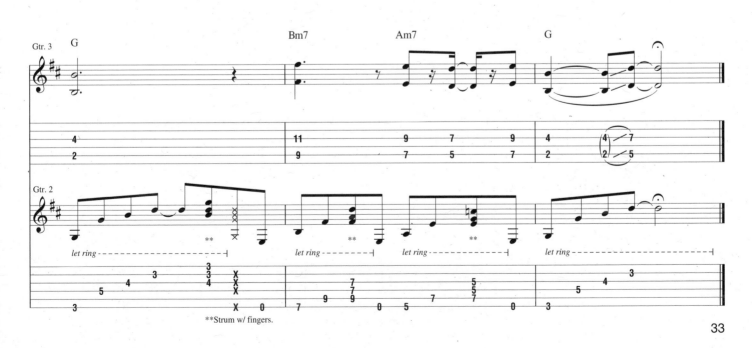

**Strum w/ fingers.

TURN YOUR LOVE

back, give it back, give it back.   Give it back. ___

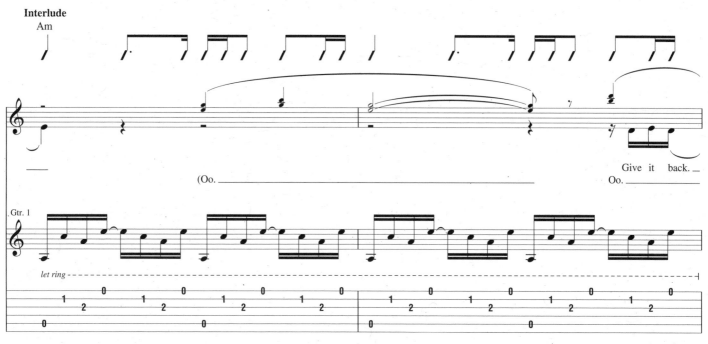

Interlude

(Oo. _____)   Give it back. ___
                                            Oo. ___

Oo.) _____   Give it

THE UPSETTER

Words and Music by
Jack Johnson

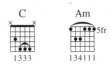

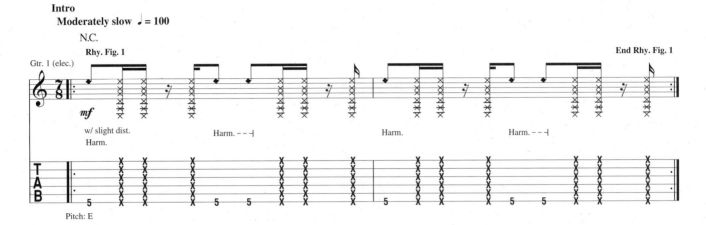

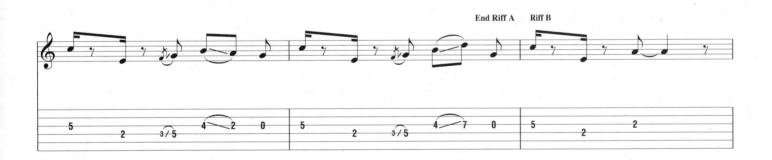

Verse

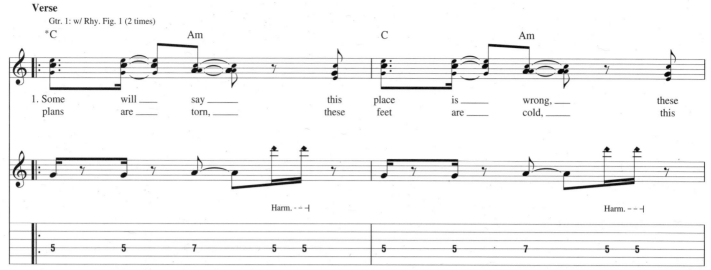

Gtr. 1: w/ Rhy. Fig. 1 (2 times)

*C   Am   C   Am

1. Some will ___ say ___ this place is ___ wrong, ___ these
plans are ___ torn, ___ these feet are ___ cold, ___ this

Harm. - - - ⌐   Harm. - - - ⌐

*Chord symbols reflect overall harmony (next 4 meas.)   Pitch: D

C   Am   C   Am

hands are ___ fast, ___ this face is ___ long. ___ Just…
shield is ___ worn, ___ this peace was ___ stol - en.

Harm. - - - ⌐   Harm. - - - ⌐

Chorus

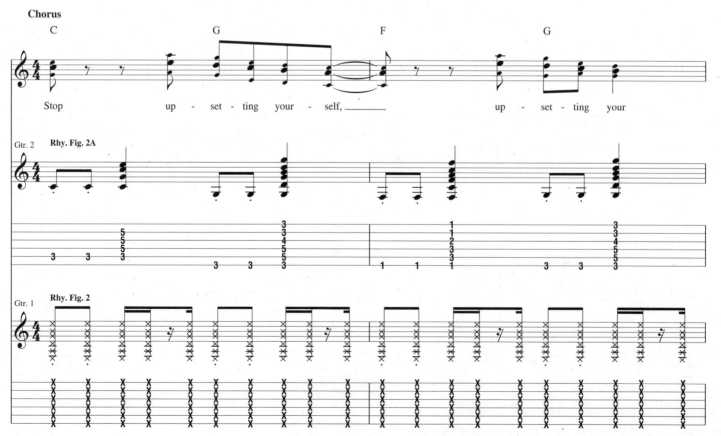

C   G   F   G

Stop up - set - ting your - self, ___ up - set - ting your

Gtr. 2   **Rhy. Fig. 2A**

Gtr. 1   **Rhy. Fig. 2**

40

Interlude

Gtr. 2: w/ Rhy. Fig. 5

Am

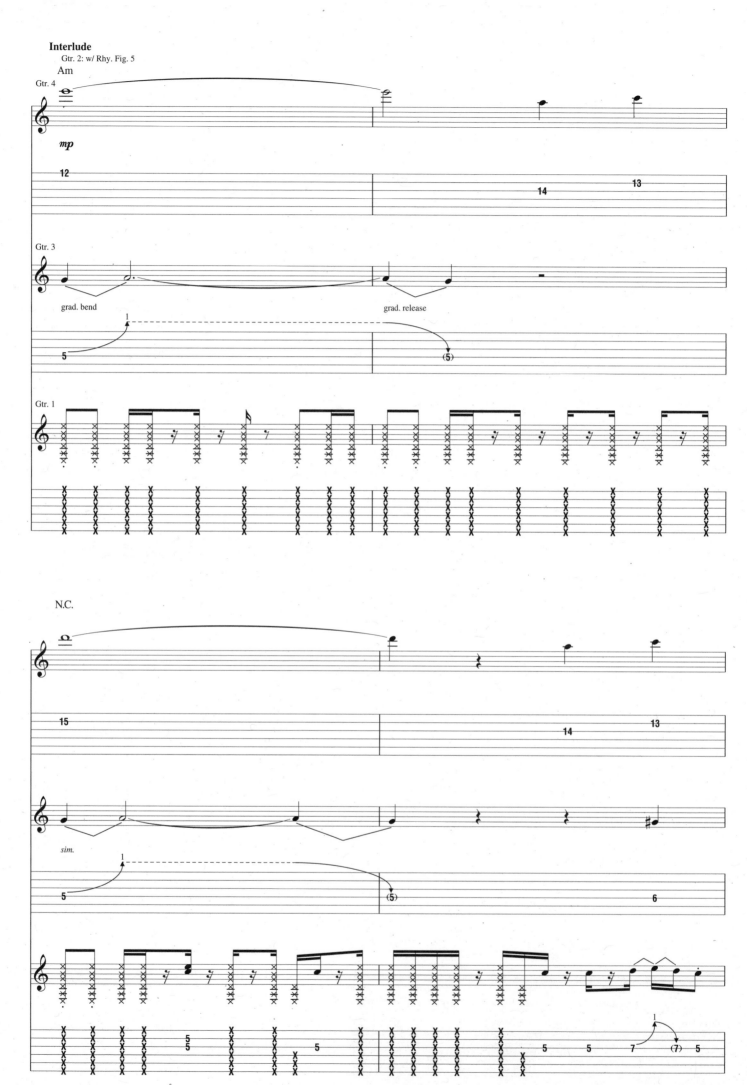

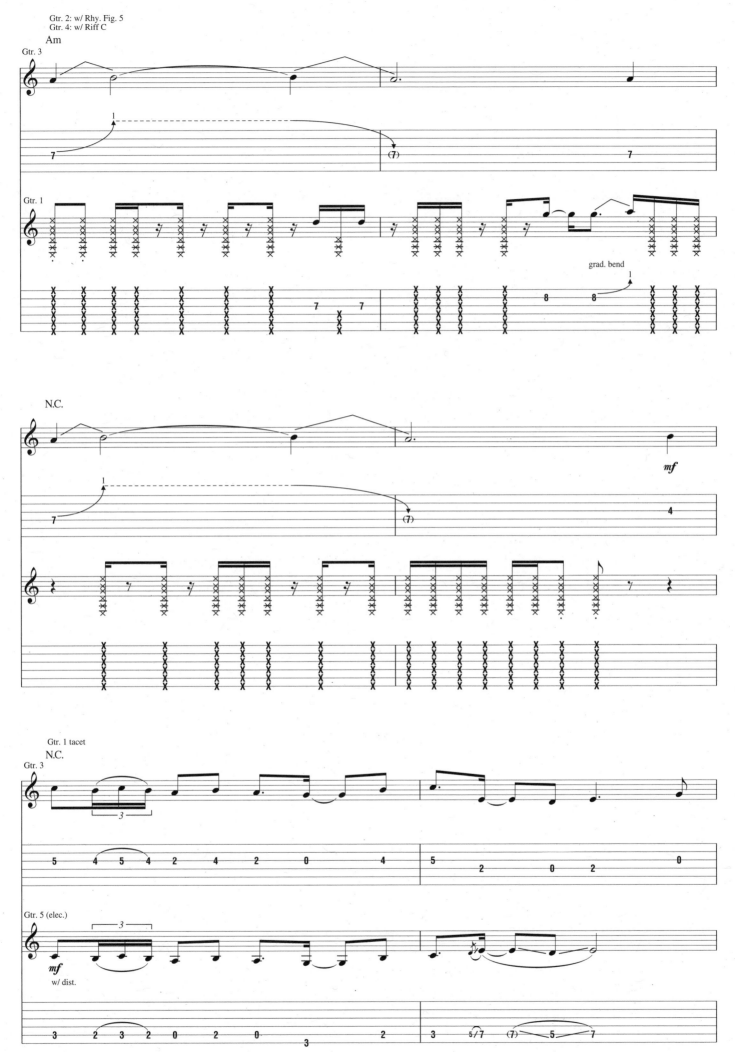

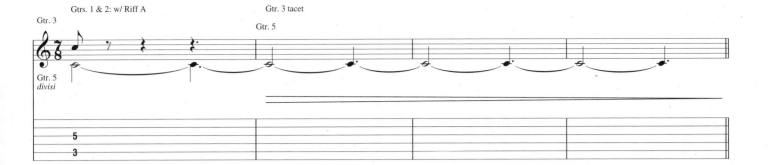

Bridge

Some will say ___ this place is gone. These roads are steep ___ and much too long. These

plans are cheap; ___ my feet are cold. Just cut the knot; ___ these coins are gold - en.

Some will say ___ this place is gone. These roads are steep ___ and much too long. (These)

plans are cheap; ___ my feet are cold. Just cut the knot; ___ these coins are gold - en.

Chorus

Stop up - set - ting your - self, ___ up - set - ting your

thoughts, up - set - ting this world ___ that you're stand - ing

on. These prob - lems, they breathe _____ and their fi - re is real. _____

_____ And the coins that they keep, _____ you can - not steal. _____

_____ E - ven when you're a - sleep, _____ they'll be _____ here still, _____

_____ just breath - ing out _____ or in.

48

RED WINE, MISTAKES, MYTHOLOGY

Words and Music by
Jack Johnson, Merlo Podlewski,
Adam Topol and Zach Gill

find the place_ where the king_ locked_ up the prin - cess, jump the fence (and) drink a lit - tle bit of...

% Chorus

Red wine, mis - takes, a - pol - o - gies.____ And it's all ___ just...

Gtr. 1   **Rhy. Fig. 1**

Gtr. 2   **Rhy. Fig. 1A**

Red wine, head - aches, my - thol - o - gy.___

(Oo, oo, oo.)

End Rhy. Fig. 1

End Rhy. Fig. 1A

What's the mat - ter? Is the feast not fat e - nough? Up the lad - der with your feet, reach - ing with your hands.__

__ You can feel it and dream it; I know you want to be - lieve it. Just steal it. Take a piece of the sun __ (and) drink some...

Coda 1

Guitar Solo

*Dyad played w/ pick & middle finger.

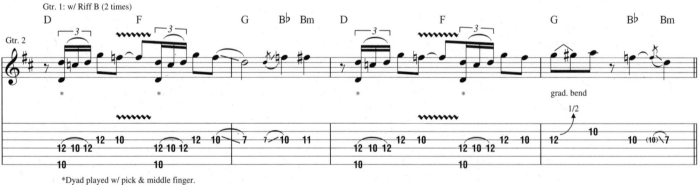

Verse

3. Now ev - 'ry - bod - y's in the play. (At) least that's __ what the script told me to say. It said,

PICTURES OF PEOPLE TAKING PICTURES

Words and Music by
Jack Johnson

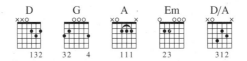

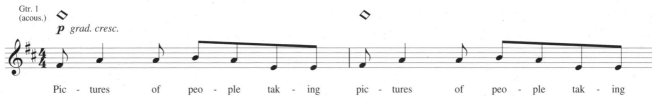

I took a pic-ture of you,___ took a pic-ture of___ me.   In the

back-ground of the pic-ture was wa - ter run-ning to the___ sea.___

𝄋 **Pre-Chorus**

Gtr. 1

So } I pic-tured us stand - ing___ there___ just,   just stay-ing a - way___
But }

___ from time.___   Just watch-ing it like___ a___ riv - er as it

slow-ly wash-es by,___   wash - es by. ___

Chorus

Rhy. Fig. 2

___   And now... Pic-tures of peo-ple tak-ing pic-tures of peo-ple tak-ing

To Coda ⊕

End Rhy. Fig. 2   Rhy. Fig. 3

pic - tures of peo - ple tak-ing pic - tures.   Pic - tures of peo - ple tak-ing

End Rhy. Fig. 3

pic - tures of peo - ple tak-ing pic - tures of peo - ple tak-ing pic - tures.   2. (The)

Verse

Gtr. 1: w/ Rhy. Fig. 1 (2 times)

A
D

feed - back loop is clos - ing in __ so __ tight, __

A
D

sur - round - ing our - selves __ with sat - el - lites. __

D.S. al Coda

Coda

Gtr. 1: w/ Rhy. Fig. 2 (last meas.)
Gtr. 1: w/ Rhy. Fig. 2 (2 times)

A
D

pic - tures and pic - tures. Pic - tures of peo - ple tak - ing pic - tures of peo - ple tak - ing

Voc. Fig. 1

(Pic - tures of peo - ple, pic - tures of

Bkgd. Voc.: w/ Voc. Fig. 1 (2 times)

A
D

pic - tures of peo - ple tak - ing pic - tures. Pic - tures of peo - ple tak - ing

End Voc. Fig. 1   Voc. Fig. 2

peo - ple, pic - tures of peo - ple tak - ing pic - tures.) (I'm so __ plas - tic, __

Bkgd. Voc.: w/ Voc. Fig. 2
Gtr. 1: w/ Rhy. Fig. 3

A
D

pic - tures of peo - ple tak - ing pic - tures of peo - ple tak - ing pic - tures. Pic - tures of peo - ple tak - ing

End Voc. Fig. 2

you're __ so __ plas - tic. Let's take __ pic - tures; __ we're __ fan - tas - tic.) (I'm so plas - tic, you're so plas - tic.

pic - tures of peo - ple tak - ing pic - tures of peo - ple tak - ing pic - tures.

Let's take pic - tures; we're fan - tas - tic. I'm so plas - tic, you're so plas - tic. Let's take pic - tures; we're fan - tas - tic.)

D
G
A

Gtr. 1

I pic - ture us __ at the end __ of time, __ tak - ing pic - tures of noth - ing.

ANYTHING BUT THE TRUTH

Words and Music by
Jack Johnson

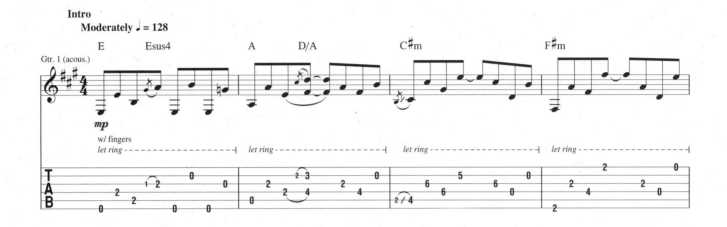

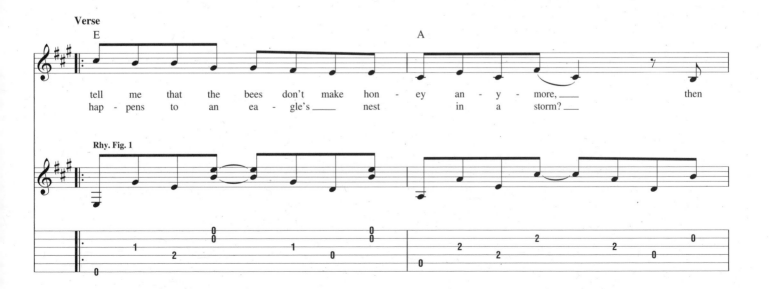

60

ONLY THE OCEAN

Words and Music by
Jack Johnson, Merlo Podlewski,
Adam Topol and Zach Gill

Gtr. 2: Capo VIII

Intro
Moderately slow ♩ = 80

*Symbols in parentheses represent chord names respective to capoed guitar.
Symbols above reflect actual sounding chords. Capoed fret is "0" in tab.
Chord symbols reflect overall harmony.

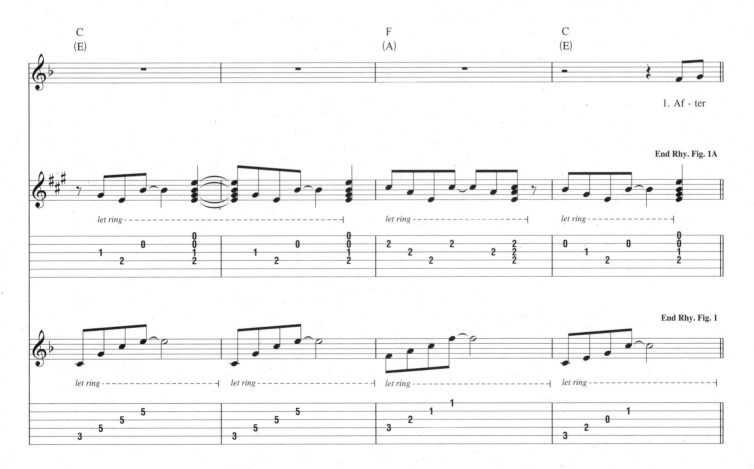

Verse

all of this time, __ af-ter all of these sea-sons, af-ter your one de-ci-sion to go to the

wa-ter for rea-son, (now) it's on-ly __ the o - cean _ and you. __ And

all of these lines __ will all be e-rased _ soon. They go out with the tide __ and come

back with the waves _ soon. It's on-ly __ the o - cean _ and you. __ You don't

Outro

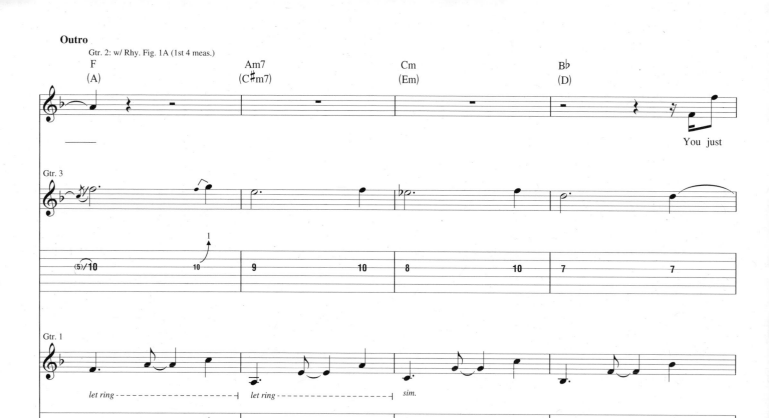

GUITAR NOTATION LEGEND

Guitar music can be notated three different ways: on a *musical staff*, in *tablature*, and in *rhythm slashes*.

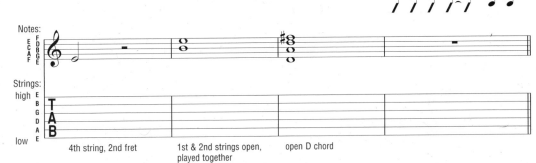

RHYTHM SLASHES are written above the staff. Strum chords in the rhythm indicated. Use the chord diagrams found at the top of the first page of the transcription for the appropriate chord voicings. Round noteheads indicate single notes.

THE MUSICAL STAFF shows pitches and rhythms and is divided by bar lines into measures. Pitches are named after the first seven letters of the alphabet.

TABLATURE graphically represents the guitar fingerboard. Each horizontal line represents a string, and each number represents a fret.

Notes:

Strings:
high E B G D A low E

4th string, 2nd fret   1st & 2nd strings open, played together   open D chord

---

HALF-STEP BEND: Strike the note and bend up 1/2 step.

WHOLE-STEP BEND: Strike the note and bend up one step.

GRACE NOTE BEND: Strike the note and immediately bend up as indicated.

SLIGHT (MICROTONE) BEND: Strike the note and bend up 1/4 step.

BEND AND RELEASE: Strike the note and bend up as indicated, then release back to the original note. Only the first note is struck.

PRE-BEND: Bend the note as indicated, then strike it.

VIBRATO: The string is vibrated by rapidly bending and releasing the note with the fretting hand.

WIDE VIBRATO: The pitch is varied to a greater degree by vibrating with the fretting hand.

HAMMER-ON: Strike the first (lower) note with one finger, then sound the higher note (on the same string) with another finger by fretting it without picking.

PULL-OFF: Place both fingers on the notes to be sounded. Strike the first note and without picking, pull the finger off to sound the second (lower) note.

LEGATO SLIDE: Strike the first note and then slide the same fret-hand finger up or down to the second note. The second note is not struck.

SHIFT SLIDE: Same as legato slide, except the second note is struck.

TRILL: Very rapidly alternate between the notes indicated by continuously hammering on and pulling off.

TAPPING: Hammer ("tap") the fret indicated with the pick-hand index or middle finger and pull off to the note fretted by the fret hand.

NATURAL HARMONIC: Strike the note while the fret-hand lightly touches the string directly over the fret indicated.

PINCH HARMONIC: The note is fretted normally and a harmonic is produced by adding the edge of the thumb or the tip of the index finger of the pick hand to the normal pick attack.

PICK SCRAPE: The edge of the pick is rubbed down (or up) the string, producing a scratchy sound.

MUFFLED STRINGS: A percussive sound is produced by laying the fret hand across the string(s) without depressing, and striking them with the pick hand.

PALM MUTING: The note is partially muted by the pick hand lightly touching the string(s) just before the bridge.

RAKE: Drag the pick across the strings indicated with a single motion.

TREMOLO PICKING: The note is picked as rapidly and continuously as possible.

VIBRATO BAR DIVE AND RETURN: The pitch of the note or chord is dropped a specified number of steps (in rhythm), then returned to the original pitch.

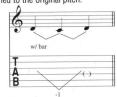

VIBRATO BAR SCOOP: Depress the bar just before striking the note, then quickly release the bar.

VIBRATO BAR DIP: Strike the note and then immediately drop a specified number of steps, then release back to the original pitch.

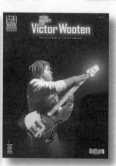